Helping Children See Jesus

ISBN: 978-1-64104-062-4

Christ Is God the Son

*New Testament Volume 34:
Hebrews, Part One*

Authors: R. Iona Lyster and Maureen Pruitt
Illustrator: Frances H. Hertzler
Colorization Courtesy of Good Life Ministries
Page Layout: Morgan Melton, Patricia Pope

© 2019 Bible Visuals International
PO Box 153, Akron, PA 17501-0153
Phone: (717) 859-1131
www.biblevisuals.org

All rights reserved. No part of this publication may be reproduced, stored in a retrieval system or transmitted in any form by any means, electronic, mechanical, photocopy, recording or otherwise, without the prior permission of the publisher, except as provided by USA copyright law.

RELATED ITEMS

To access related items (such as activities, memory verse posters and translated texts) please visit our webstore at www.biblevisuals.org and enter 1034 in the search box on the page.

FREE TEXT DOWNLOAD

To access a FREE printable copy of the teaching text (PDF format) in English or other available languages, enter S1034DL in the search box. Add the item to your cart, and use coupon code XTACSV17 at checkout. Once your order is processed you will receive an email with a link to the free download.

STUDENT ACTIVITES

These are included with the FREE printable copy of the English teaching text for this story. See the directions under Free Text Download (above) to access them.

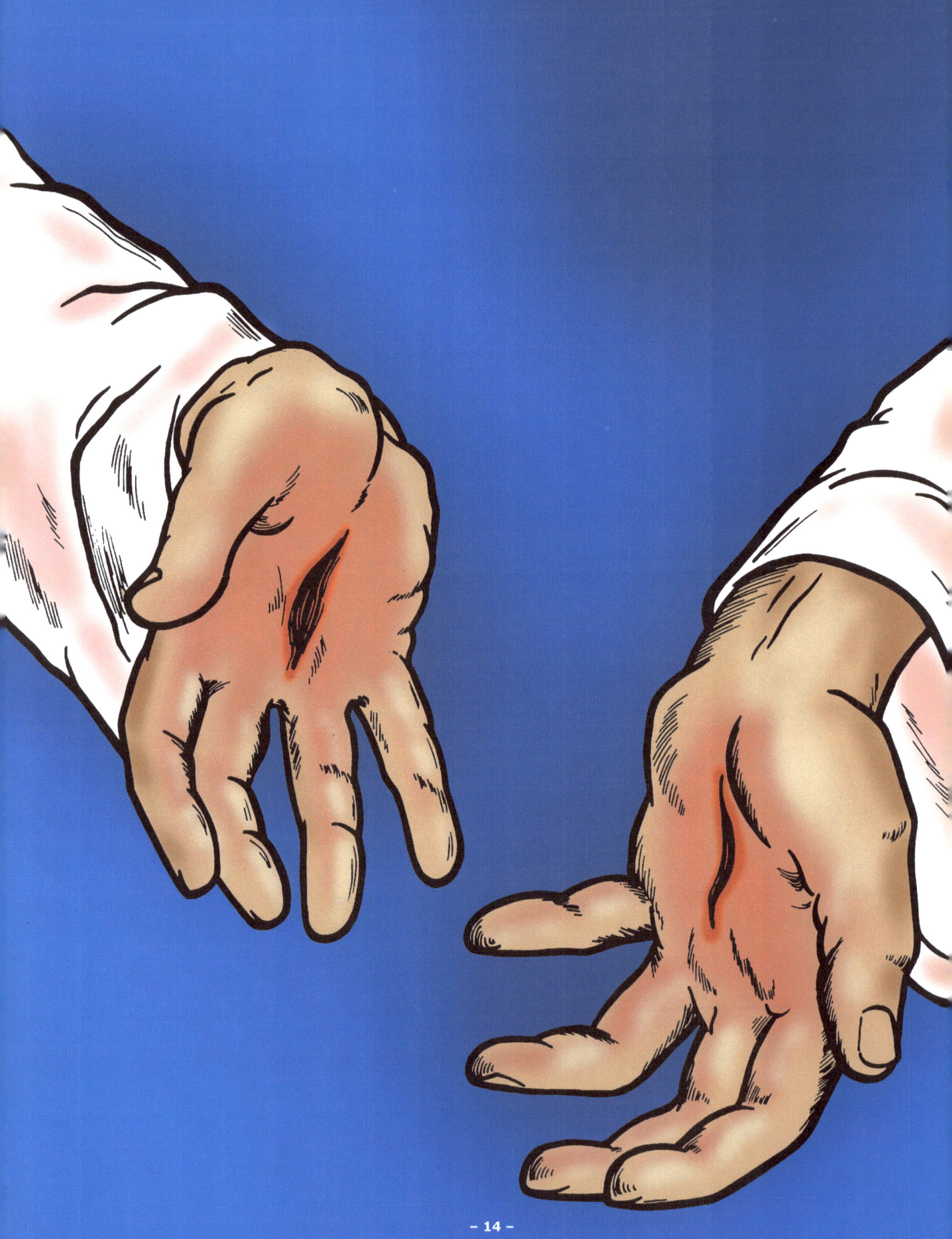

Jesus Christ

the same yesterday, and to day, and forever.

Hebrews 13:8

Lesson 1
CHRIST IS BETTER THAN ANGELS

NOTE TO THE TEACHER

There has been much discussion as to who wrote the letter addressed to the Hebrews (another name for the Jewish people). Perhaps the name of the author was purposely hidden so the Holy Spirit could reveal the Son alone as the final message and messenger of God. (See Hebrews 1:2.)

We are not told the location of the church (or churches) addressed in the letter. We do know, however, that the readers were Jewish people who had turned to the Lord Jesus. Probably, as in churches today, there were some who said they were Christians but were not genuinely born again. However, most of them would have been true believers ("holy brethren," 3:1) who suffered for their faith in Christ (10:32b). Alas, these Jewish Christians were having problems. As Christians, they could no longer worship at the majestic temple. Like many Christians in that day, they were afraid of being persecuted. So, instead of advancing with purpose in their spiritual lives, they were floundering uncertainly.

So the Spirit of God directed this letter to them. They were warned not to come short, not to be slothful, not to sin willfully and not to draw back. Watch for these warnings as you study.

In this series we have five volumes on the book of Hebrews:

1. Christ Is God the Son
2. Eternal Salvation
3. The Priesthood of Christ
4. The New Covenant
5. Living by Faith

Scripture to be studied: Hebrews 1:4-14; Psalm 2:7; 45:6-7; 102:25-27; 104:4; 110:1

The *aim* of the lesson: To show that Christ is greater than angels.

What your students should *know*: Although angels are the messengers of God, Christ is God the Son.

What your students should *feel*: A desire to give Christ the highest place.

What your students should *do*: Worship the One whom angels worship: Christ the Son of God.

Lesson outline (for the teacher's and students' notebooks):

1. Christ has a better name than angels (Hebrews 1:4-5).
2. Christ is worshiped by angels (Hebrews 1:6).
3. Christ will rule over all of God's kingdom (Hebrews 1:7-9, 13-14).
4. Christ created everything (Hebrews 1:10-12).

The verse to be memorized:

Jesus Christ the same yesterday, and to day, and forever.
(Hebrews 13:8)

THE LESSON

The Bible has a great deal to say about angels. It records many things which they did. For example, they announced the birth of the Lord Jesus. What else did they do? Who sent them? Why did angels appear? (*Teacher:* Encourage class discussion.)

God created many thousands of angels. (See Psalm 68:17; Matthew 26:53; Hebrews 12:22; Revelation 5:11.) They do His work in the heavens and can carry His messages to people on earth. Although they are spiritual beings, on occasion they are able to look like men. (See Genesis 19:1, 5; Numbers 22:22-31; Judges 6:11, 22; 13:3, 6.) They have tremendous power and strength (2 Kings 19:35; Matthew 28:2). Yet they tenderly watch over the children of God. (See Psalm 91:11; Matthew 18:10; Hebrews 1:14.) The Epistle to the Hebrews, which we will be studying, has much to say about angels, as we'll see in today's lesson.

We aren't told what the Jewish Christians said when they received the letter addressed to them. However, we believe that in at least one family, it may have been like this:

Because of his position in the church, Benaiah had been allowed to take home the letter written to the Hebrews. Each night he sat close to the little oil light studying every sentence carefully. Occasionally he frowned, as if he couldn't understand the message. Often he looked as though he had been scolded. Finally one night he called his oldest son aside. "Eliab," he began, "you're young. But I have to confess something to you. I 've not been living the right kind of Christian life."

Eliab was amazed. He had never heard his father admit doing any wrong.

Benaiah continued, "When you were only a baby, Eliab, your mother and I turned to the Lord Jesus Christ and received Him as Saviour. After that, everything was different. We prayed differently. We worshiped God in a new way. And, as you know, many who are not Christians have tormented all of us. Once they were our friends. Now they hate us. It is nice to meet with the other Christians in homes. But I miss the worship we enjoyed at the magnificent temple."

"I have never been inside the temple," Eliab said sadly.

"I know, my son. I know. And it's a great pity. You can't know how I have longed to take you there." He continued, "I love the Lord Jesus. And I shall always be thankful for the day your mother and I placed our trust in Him. But lately I've been wanting the old things, too. Now, since the Spirit of God has directed a letter to us Jews, I see how wrong I've been."

"Wrong in what way, Father?" Eliab wanted to know.

1. CHRIST HAS A BETTER NAME THAN ANGELS
Hebrews 1:4-5

"Well, for example, I have been thinking a great deal about angels. Our Jewish history is filled with experiences our people had with angels. Indeed, angels are of such importance that we Jews have respected them, shown them reverence, even prayed to them. And to my shame, now that I'm a Christian I've been giving them too much thought and attention. God has rebuked me in this letter. He has shown me that the Lord Jesus Christ is far better, far greater than all the angels. From the Old Testament Scriptures which we Jews know, God shows in this letter why Christ is above angels. He begins by saying that Christ has a better name."

Show Illustration #1

(*Teacher:* In the rays, please print the words: "This is My beloved Son.")

Eliab was confused. "How can Christ's name make Him higher than angels?"

Benaiah explained, "The name *angel* means *messenger*. But God speaks of Christ as His Son. Which is of more importance? A messenger of God or the Son of God?"

"The Son," Eliab answered.

"Of course. Now remember this: God spoke of the Lord Jesus as His Son long before Christ came to earth. (See Psalm 2:7; 2 Samuel 7:14; compare Hebrews 1:5.) He was with the Father always. When Christ came to earth, God opened the heavens twice and announced for all to hear, 'This [Jesus] is My beloved Son.' " (See Matthew 3:17; 17:5.)

"Oh, I see," Eliab said brightly. "Because the Lord Jesus is the Son of God, He is better than angels."

"Exactly. But there's more. God says Christ inherited a more excellent name than angels. An inheritance is something a son receives from his father. The Lord Jesus received from His Father God His authority and His excellence. These are included in the word *name*. We use this idea often. I say to you, 'Do not bring disgrace upon our family name.' And you know I am speaking of our reputation, our manner of life, our character."

"Oh, I understand!" Eliab exclaimed. "Because the Lord Jesus is named the Son of God, He is better than angels."

2. CHRIST IS WORSHIPED BY ANGELS
Hebrews 1:6

"Yes, and there's more in this letter to us Hebrews," Benaiah continued. "But let me ask you a question: Who receives worship? One who is important or the One who is God?"

"God," Eliab answered correctly.

Show Illustration #2

"Exactly. God reminds us of something He said long ago: 'Let all the angels of God worship Him' [the Lord Jesus] (Hebrews 1:6). Angels have doubtless been doing this ever since they were created. They surely worshiped the Lord Jesus while He was in Heaven. Certainly they worshiped Him when they announced His coming to earth. They worshiped Him when one of their number declared His resurrection. They worshiped Him when He returned to the Father in Heaven. And a day will come when we will join with the angels and worship Him." (See Philippians 2:9-11; Revelation 5:11-12. (*Teacher:* Although Revelation was written after Hebrews, we believe the Jewish Christians knew the truth mentioned in Revelation 5:11-12.)

Eliab said thoughtfully, "Christ the Son has a better name than angels. He has the nature of God. And angels do worship Him. So He is better than angels."

"Yes," his father said encouragingly. "But there is more."

3. CHRIST WILL RULE OVER ALL OF GOD'S KINGDOM
Hebrews 1:7-9, 13-14

Show Illustration #3

Benaiah continued, "The Spirit of God speaks in this letter of something else He said in the book of Psalms. There He mentioned that the angels are spirit beings who do His work. (See Psalm 104:4.) They are only servants. But God said to Jesus before He came to earth: 'Thy throne, O God, is forever and ever' (Psalm 45:6-7). Think of that! God Himself calls His Son God. So the Lord Jesus is not only the Son of God. He is God. Angels are simply His servants."

"No wonder He is better than angels," Eliab declared.

"In addition, this One whom angels worship reigns as King forever. It says in our letter, 'Thy throne, O God, is forever and ever: a scepter of uprightness is the scepter of Thy kingdom.' The Lord Jesus is in Heaven now, sitting on His Father's throne. (See Hebrews 1:13; Psalm 110:1.) The earth, the sun, the moon and stars are held by His power. (See Colossians 1:16-17.) Later, when all His enemies are defeated (See Hebrews 1:13.), the Lord Jesus will reign forever from His own throne. (See Matthew 25:31.) Until then, He is sitting alongside His Father, while the angels serve Him."

"Christ surely is much, much higher than angels, isn't He?"

"Yes, Eliab. And I am glad we have this letter. Otherwise I might have gone back to angel worship again."

4. CHRIST CREATED EVERYTHING
Hebrews 1:10-12

Show Illustration #4

Tugging his beard thoughtfully, Benaiah added, "God reminds us that the Lord Jesus was with Him in the beginning, creating everything. (See Hebrews 1:10; Psalm 102:25; John 1:3; Colossians 1:16.) He created the heavens. He created the earth, the sun, the moon and the stars. He created animals and fish. He created man and woman. He created everything and that includes angels!"

Eliab sat thinking. Finally he said, "The One who creates angels is surely greater than the angels He creates."

"You are exactly right, son. Never let that truth slip from you. Angels are important. But the Lord Jesus Christ is far more important. To help us remember why this is so, let's write down what we've learned from this letter."

Together the father and son wrote:

1. Christ has a better name than angels. He is the Son of God. Angels are messengers of God.
2. Christ is worshiped by angels, because He is God.
3. Christ will rule over all of God's kingdom. He is God the Son. Angels are His servants.
4. Christ created everything including angels.

(*Teacher:* Urge your students to write these truths in their notebooks.)

Is it perfectly clear to you that the Lord Jesus is greater and higher than all the angels? If angels worship Him, we who are lower than angels should certainly worship Him. Do you worship Him? Have you given Him the right place in your life? He is the Son of God. He is God the Son.

Just stop to think of it! Though He is so great, yet He came to die for you and me, that He might bring us this wonderful salvation. Have you placed all your trust in Him?

Lesson 2
CHRIST IS BETTER THAN THE PROPHETS

NOTE TO THE TEACHER

God promised, more than seven hundred years before Christ was born, that His name would be "Immanuel." (See Isaiah 7:14.) What a name! What wonderful meaning it has: *God with us*. (See Matthew 1:23.) Throughout all the ages of eternity, God knew He would come to earth in a human body. He would come for one purpose: to save His people from their sins. (See Matthew 1:21.)

Can God–the holy One–be with us? Is it possible for God, the maker of the heavens and the earth, to take on a human body? Can the One who owns all the worlds be the One who said of Himself, "The foxes have holes, and the birds of the air have nests; but the Son of Man hath not where to lay his head"? (See Matthew 8:20.) He's the One before whom all creatures shall bow, confessing Him as Lord. How could He allow men to spit in His face and nail Him to a cross? We may never understand these truths. But God's Word tells us they are so, and His Word is true.

The prophets (mentioned in the opening verse of Hebrews) are messengers of God. Some of them unveiled the future. Others did not. But all of them wrote or spoke for God, guided by the Holy Spirit. (See 2 Peter 1:21.) The prophets revealed the messages of God. But the Lord Jesus revealed God Himself. Surely the Son of God is far greater than the prophets!

Scripture to be studied: Hebrews 1:1-3; John 1:1-14, 18; Colossians 1:12-20

The *aim* of the lesson: To prove that Christ is better than the prophets.

What your students should *know*: That everything which the prophets promised about Christ is true.

What your students should *feel*: Gratitude that God Himself came to earth as a Man.

What your students should *do*:
Unsaved: Place their trust in the Saviour.
Saved: Give Christ the highest place in their lives.

Lesson outline (for the teacher's and students' notebooks):
1. At first, God spoke directly to man (Genesis 3:8-19).
2. Later, God spoke to men through the prophets (Hebrews 1:1).
3. Today, God speaks through His Son (Hebrews 1:2).
4. Jesus Christ is God with us (Hebrews 1:2-3; Isaiah 7:14; Matthew 1:23).

The verse to be memorized:

Jesus Christ the same yesterday, and to day, and forever.
(Hebrews 13:8)

THE LESSON

Have you ever seen a prophet? According to the Bible, what is a prophet? (*Teacher:* Encourage class discussion.) Who is more important: a prophet (messenger) of God, or God Himself? Let's see what the letter to the Hebrews says about this.

We have no way of knowing exactly what happened when the Jewish people read the letter addressed to them. Perhaps different ones took turns taking it home and studying it there. Some of the men in the church may have had a meeting that went like this:

1. AT FIRST, GOD SPOKE DIRECTLY TO MAN
Genesis 3:8-19

Eldest Brother began, "This letter begins abruptly, without even a word of greeting. But I like it. We're reminded at once that God has spoken bit by bit (*sundry times*) for hundreds of years. He spoke through dreams and visions; He spoke through thunderings and a still, small voice; He spoke through angels and men. He spoke differently (*in divers manners*) at various times. But He has spoken to His people. How different He is from the gods of wood and stone! They have mouths, but they cannot speak. They are silent gods. They have no life. The true God is alive and has always wanted to speak to His own."

Show Illustration #5

Younger Brother added, "In the very beginning He spoke directly to people on earth. When He talked to Adam, He asked him to give names to all the animals God had created. He told Adam to take care of the garden He had provided for them."

Eldest Brother continued, "Yes, and God told Adam they could eat all the fruit they wanted, except from one tree. That was the tree of the knowledge of good and evil. But Eve and Adam both disobeyed God. And that broke the companionship they had enjoyed."

"It's interesting, though," Younger Brother observed, "that God always wanted to talk with His people. Even after sin spoiled things, God still spoke to men and women, and children, too."

2. LATER, GOD SPOKE TO MEN THROUGH THE PROPHETS
Hebrews 1:1

Eldest Brother stood up stiffly, stretched his legs and limped back and forth. "I was just thinking," he began, "how good God has been to us Hebrews. Not all of our ancestors heard God's voice. But they all heard His message. If He didn't speak to them personally, He spoke to them through prophets, His messengers. See, that's what it says here in our letter: " 'God… spoke in time past to the fathers by the prophets.' "

Youngest Brother asked, "What kind of messages did God give to the prophets?"

– 20 –

Show Illustration #6

"Sometimes He told them to warn people of their sin and of punishment if they continued sinning. The Prophet Jonah, for example, went up and down the streets of the wicked city of Nineveh crying, 'In forty days Nineveh shall be overthrown.' When the Ninevites heard that, they all repented of their sin from the king down to the least person in the kingdom. They not only repented, they turned from their evil. So God forgave them. And they were not destroyed. Why? Because they obeyed God's warning given through His prophet." (See Jonah 3:1-10.)

Another elder spoke up, saying, "Some of the prophets told of the glorious kingdom which God will set up on earth some day. Zechariah the prophet said, 'The LORD shall be King over all the earth' (Zechariah 14:9). I wonder when that day will come."

3. TODAY, GOD SPEAKS THROUGH HIS SON
Hebrews 1:2

Eldest Brother declared, "We don't know when His Kingdom will come. But we know it will come, for God Himself said so. But there were other messages which God gave through the prophets. Many of them spoke of the One whom God would send to earth to reveal more about God and His Kingdom. Hundreds of years, even thousands before He came, God promised He would come."

Show Illustration #7

Stroking his beard thoughtfully, Eldest Brother continued, "I'm very ashamed of us Hebrews. Our prophets were perfectly clear about the One whom God would send. The Prophet Micah said He would be born in King David's city, the city of Bethlehem. (See Micah 5:2.) Our people had known this for seven hundred years. Then one day God opened the heavens and announced through angels, 'Unto you is born this day in the City of David a Saviour, who is Christ the Lord' (Luke 2:11). We should have understood at once that this was the promised One from God. But it took us a long, long time to recognize Him. And many of our Jewish friends still do not believe He has come."

Another elder added, "And then the Prophet Isaiah said His mother would be unmarried. He even foretold one of His names, when he wrote: 'Behold, a virgin shall conceive, and bear a Son, and shall call His name *Immanuel* (Isaiah 7:14). And this is exactly what happened. (See Matthew 1:18-25.) The Lord Jesus came in a miraculous way. He had no earthly father. He did speak of His heavenly Father saying, 'I and My Father are One' (John 10:30). When He said this, our people picked up stones to stone Him. I wonder why we were so blind to the writings of our prophets."

"Do you remember what the Prophet Zechariah wrote?" Elder Brother asked.

Without waiting for an answer, he continued, "Zechariah said the promised One would ride into the city of Jerusalem on an ass and its colt. (See Zechariah 9:9.) Five hundred years later, Christ did that. Seeing Him, our people joined the crowds who shouted, 'Blessed is He who comes in the name of the Lord' (Matthew 21:9). Yet only a few days later we demanded, 'Crucify Him!' How could we have been so ignorant?"

Another elder said, "It would be interesting to learn how God finally got His message through to all of us. For me, it was the first sermon which Peter, a Jew, preached. He reminded us that our ancestor, David, had told us that God would not let His Holy One stay in the grave. Nor would He let His body decay. (See Acts 2:27; Psalm 16:10.) Peter explained that David was speaking of the resurrection of Christ. He concluded his sermon to us Jews saying, 'God has made this Jesus both Lord and Christ! He is the One you nailed to a cross!' (See Acts 2:36.) I was one of the thousands who turned to the Lord Jesus that day. I am thankful for the holy men who have delivered God's messages to our people. (See 2 Peter 1:21.) Without them I could never have been certain that the Lord Jesus Christ is the Son of God."

"It's true that we owe a great deal to the messengers of God," Eldest Brother agreed. "But look what it says in our letter. Instead of speaking His messages through prophets, God now speaks to us in His Son. The prophets wrote: 'The Lord says' but Christ spoke with authority: 'I say to you.' (See Matthew 5:20, 22, 26, 28, 32, 34, 39, 44.) (*Teacher:* It may be well to read these accounts to your students.) And God Himself spoke from Heaven twice saying 'This is My beloved Son, in whom I am well pleased.' (See Matthew 3:17; 17:5.) Once God added, 'Hear ye Him.' So, whatever the Son of God says, is final. We are to listen to Him."

4. JESUS CHRIST IS GOD WITH US
Hebrews 1:2-3; Isaiah 7:14; Matthew 1:23

Eldest Brother continued, "As you know, some of us have been unfaithful in our Christian lives. We haven't always given the Lord Jesus Christ His rightful place. But listen to what God says about Christ. (*Teacher:* Encourage students to pick out the truths of Hebrews 1:2-3.) God has put all things into Christ's hands making Him Lord of everything. Christ was with the Father creating everything. (Compare John 1:1-3; Ephesians 3:9; Colossians 1:16.) Christ is the shining brightness of God. Christ reveals exactly what God is like. Christ is the One who holds everything together. Now listen to this, brothers!" Eldest Brother commanded attention.

Show Illustration #8

"This One who is far higher, far greater than we can understand took care of our sins. The prophets, great as they were, offered the blood of lambs as sacrifices for their sins. Christ gave His own blood. He, the Lord of Heaven and earth, became the Lamb of God and died for the sins of the world. He died in our place. After He gave Himself, He sat down beside God."

Younger Brother spoke up, "No one ever sits down in the presence of a king."

"That's true," Eldest Brother agreed. "But if that person is equal with the king, he may sit with him. And this is exactly what we are to understand from this letter. The Lord Jesus Christ, Son of God, is equal with God. (See Philippians 2:6.) Indeed, He is God with us. For that's what His name, *Immanuel*, means. Whatever God is, He is. By looking at Christ, we know exactly what God is like."

The men had lots to think about. Did they memorize the first three verses of Hebrews? (Remember, please, that the letter was not broken into verses until long years later.) Did they copy the verses so they could have them for themselves? We don't know. Do you suppose the men shared with their families the truths they had learned? What questions would their families have asked? What do you imagine they said in their prayers that night? (*Teacher:* Encourage your group to discuss what the Hebrew Christians may have done after reading the opening part of the letter.)

There are Jews living in almost every country of the world. Suppose you were to meet a Jewish person, one who has never believed in the Lord Jesus Christ. Could you show him what the Jewish prophets say about Christ?

What glorious truths about Christ could you show him from the book of Hebrews? (*Teacher:* Try to get your students to mention the seven facts of Hebrews 1:2-3. If possible, have them list these truths in their notebooks.)

Do you know someone who is not Jewish who should hear about Christ? Would you like us to pray for that person right now?

If you have never placed your trust in the Saviour, will you do it now? He has paid for your sins with His own precious blood. He is waiting to forgive you and will give you everlasting life when you receive Him.

Lesson 3
CHRIST IS BETTER THAN MOSES

NOTE TO THE TEACHER

God promised to guide His people out of slavery in Egypt into a wonderful land of their own. He used Moses to lead them. When the people finally got to the border of their promised land, God said, "Go in." But, because they were afraid, the people refused. They didn't trust God fully. And God punished them by making them wander in the wilderness for 40 years. (See Numbers 14:33-35.) Once, Moses didn't follow God's instructions exactly. (See Numbers 20:7-12.) So God said, "You can't go into the land, Moses. Joshua will lead the people in." What a disappointment for Moses!

What did Moses do? Instead of feeling sorry for himself, he trained Joshua, the man who replaced him. He encouraged and strengthened Joshua. (See Deuteronomy 1:38; 3:28.)

It takes God-given love and humility to train those who will replace us. God's command to us, as to Moses, is to strengthen, train and encourage those who will be future leaders. Ask the Lord to help you in this, teacher.

Scripture to be studied: Hebrews 2:14-17; 3:1–4:11; 4:14-16; 11:23-29; Exodus 2 and 12; Acts 7:17-36

The *aim* of the lesson: To show that Christ is greater than Moses.

What your students should *know*: That Christ perfectly meets all their needs.

What your students should *feel*: Gratitude for deliverance from Satan's slavery.

What your students should *do*:
Saved: Confess any disobedience to God. Seek to obey Him every day.
Unsaved: Place their trust in the Saviour today.

Lesson outline (for the teacher's and students' notebooks):
1. God gives a deliverer (Hebrews 3:1-6).
2. God rescues by blood (Hebrews 2:14-17).
3. God meets daily needs (Hebrews 3:14; 4:14-16).
4. God has special blessings for those who believe Him (Hebrews 3:15-4:11).

The verse to be memorized:

Jesus Christ the same yesterday, and to day, and forever.
(Hebrews 13:8)

THE LESSON

Have you ever had a hero? Maybe it was someone important. Maybe not. But to you, he/she was the greatest person anywhere. You wanted to know everything about that person. What did you do in order to learn all you could about your hero? (*Teacher:* Encourage class discussion.)

For hundreds of years the Jewish people have had a hero. His name is Moses. He was especially popular at the time the Spirit of God addressed a letter to the Hebrew Christians. (That was more than 1900 years ago.) Angels and prophets and Moses were of great importance to the Jews. So it is not surprising that God had much to say about each of these in Hebrews.

You must remember there was only one copy of the letter at that time. So the men may have passed it from one to another. Many who were younger might have memorized much of it. Everyone, from the oldest to the youngest, was eager to learn all that was written to them. Maybe when the children and young people got together, the talk went like this:

1. GOD GIVES A DELIVERER
Hebrews 3:1-6

"Moses has always been my hero," Eliab began. "All kinds of interesting things happened to him. His life was one long adventure. Why, when he was only three months old he was placed among the bulrushes in the river all alone in a little covered boat. That must have been great!"

Show Illustration #9

"But Moses' mother was scared," a girl declared. "She had been hiding him from the day he was born so the king of Egypt wouldn't kill him. Finally she had to put him into the river, hoping someone would find him and take care of him."

"And it was the princess, the king's daughter, who found Moses," Eliab added. "She rescued the baby and later took him to live with her in the palace. Imagine that! Moses lived right with the king who had commanded that he and all the Hebrew baby boys should be killed. So God outsmarted the devil!"

"It was one of God's miracles," Marcus added. "A miracle like the one He used hundreds of years later to save the life of the Lord Jesus. When He came to earth, His mother placed Him in a manger bed. Shortly after His birth, God sent an angel to Joseph, saying, 'Get up! Take the young Child and His mother, and go into Egypt. Stay there until I bring you word. For King Herod will try to kill the Child.' Joseph obeyed God, and Christ was kept safe. If a miracle is needed to take care of one whom He loves, God will do that miracle."

Eliab spoke again. "I guess that is why Moses is my hero. His life seemed to be one miracle after another. For example, even though he was a Jew, he got the best Egyptian training right in the palace. He could have been a ruler of that land.

Instead he chose to help free our Hebrew people who were slaves of the Egyptians. (See Hebrews 11:24-27.) But the Jews didn't understand what he wanted to do. And he had to escape from the palace and hide in the desert. There he stayed for 40 years, learning about desert life."

Reuben added, "When it comes to miracles, how do you like this one? One day in the desert a bush was on fire. But it didn't burn up. Instead Someone spoke to Moses out of the bush. It was the Lord God Himself who said, 'Take off your shoes, Moses. The place where you are standing is holy. I am going to deliver My people, the Jews, from the Egyptians. And I will use you to be their leader.' God was pleased with Moses and spoke to him as we speak to our friends." (See Exodus 33:11.)

"It is true that God spoke to Moses as a friend," Marcus began. "However, in the letter we have just received, God says that 'Moses was faithful…as a servant . . . but Christ . . . as a Son . . .' (Hebrews 3:5-6). While the Lord Jesus was here on earth, God announced from Heaven: 'This is My beloved Son, in whom I am well pleased. Listen to Him.' Moses was a servant of God, and that is good. But Christ is the Son of God. And that is much better."

2. GOD RESCUES BY BLOOD
Hebrews 2:14-17

Eliab could not sit still. He jumped up, saying, "God really made a great leader out of Moses. His 40 years of training in the palace helped him, too."

Eliab continued, "God did all kinds of miracles through Moses. The last one in Egypt has to be one of the greatest."

"Which one was that?" a wide-eyed girl wanted to know.

Show Illustration #10

Eliab answered, "God told Moses to have each Jewish family kill a lamb which had no defects and put its blood on the doorway of their home. God promised, 'When I see the blood, I will pass over.' At midnight, the death angel went from house to house. And God protected all the Jewish families who had blood on their doorways. But the oldest son in each Egyptian family was killed because there was no blood on their homes. That terrified the king of Egypt. So he finally allowed our Jewish people (and there were many thousands of them!) to leave his land. (See Exodus 12:37-38.) And Moses led them all. What a man!"

"It is true that Moses was a great leader," Marcus agreed. "But Moses was not able to set the people free by himself. Thousands of lambs had to die before the Egyptian king would release our ancestors from slavery. Today all people everywhere are slaves of someone much worse than the king of Egypt. They are slaves of sin and of Satan. Because this is so, God came to earth as a Man, the Man Christ Jesus. He, *Immanuel* (God with us), became flesh and blood just as we are flesh and blood." (See Hebrews 2:14.)

As a perfect Lamb (See John 1:29.) Jesus took upon Himself once for all the sin of the whole world. Our prophet Isaiah foretold He would do this. (See Isaiah 53:6; compare 1 Peter 2:24.) By His death, He, by Himself, paid the punishment for our sins. (See Hebrews 1:3; 9:26.) But because He is God the Son, He came back from the dead and lives forevermore. Now, all who put their trust in Him are set free from the power of sin and Satan. Moses was a great man, but he couldn't do anything like that. The Lord Jesus Christ is far greater than Moses!"

3. GOD MEETS DAILY NEEDS
Hebrews 3:14; 4:14-16

Eliab frowned. Then he brightened, saying, "How about the forty years Moses led the people through the wilderness? Remember how God used him to do great things for our people? There were thousands and thousands of men and women and children. And who knows how many animals? But there was no water anywhere."

Show Illustration #11

"So God told Moses to hit a rock. When he did, streams of water gushed out. And everyone had plenty to drink. Imagine doing that kind of miracle!"

Marcus agreed, "That was tremendous! Now listen to this. The Lord Jesus said, 'Whoever drinks the water that I will give him will never thirst…the water I give him will be in him a well of water springing up into everlasting life.' (See John 4:13-14.) Having water to keep our mouths from being dry is good. To have living water, God's everlasting life, is far better!"

Eliab retorted, "When the people were hungry, Moses asked God for bread. The next morning and for years God rained down from Heaven a special kind of food: manna. Those thousands of people had all the fresh bread they needed. How do you like that for a king-size miracle?"

"That was a marvelous thing," Marcus said assuringly. "Do you want to hear what the Lord Jesus said about it?" Not waiting for an answer, Marcus continued, "Jesus said, 'Moses didn't give you that bread from Heaven; but My Father gives you the true bread from Heaven. For the bread of God, is He who comes down from Heaven and gives life to the world. . . . I am the bread of life: he that comes to Me shall never hunger. . . . I am the living bread which came down from Heaven: if any man eat of this bread, he shall live forever.' (See John 6:32-33, 35, 51.) God gave daily bread in the desert. But He gives eternal life through Christ. If you could choose one or the other, which would you rather have?"

Eliab did not answer. He was too busy thinking. "Remember when the people of Israel complained because they didn't have meat?" he asked. "Moses prayed and God said He would send meat that night. And He did: flocks of quails (birds). Thousands of them!"

"But listen to what the Lord Jesus said," Marcus insisted. "Labor . . . for that meat which endures unto everlasting life, which the Son of Man shall give you. Then Christ urged people to believe on Him. (See John 6:27, 29.) Having everlasting life is a lot better than simply having meat to eat. However, as long as we are on this earth, our physical bodies will need water and bread and meat. As God provided for His people in the wilderness, He provides our needs today. (See Matthew 6:31-33.) In addition, all who have placed their trust in Christ receive His life: everlasting life. Moses could not give everlasting life to anybody. The Lord Jesus is far, far above Moses. Do you agree?" he asked the group.

"Yes." "Yes." "Yes." It was perfectly clear to everyone, including Eliab, that Christ is better than Moses.

4. GOD HAS SOMETHING SPECIAL FOR THOSE WHO BELIEVE HIM
Hebrews 3:15–4:11

Marcus continued, "Our people could have gone into that wonderful land God had for them in a rather short time. (See

Deuteronomy 1:2.) But instead, they wandered in the wilderness for 40 long years."

"Why?" a wide-awake girl wanted to know.

"Because they sinned," Marcus explained. "They had been slaves in Egypt, wretched, over-worked, exhausted slaves. They could have had rest and lots of good things to eat if they had believed God. He told them that the wonderful land He had prepared for them was theirs. All they had to do was march in and take it. But they were afraid and refused to obey God. So He punished them by letting all but two of the grown-ups die in the wilderness. Only the young got into the land." (See Numbers 13:17–14:45; Deuteronomy 1:20-45.)

"What a pity!" Eliab exclaimed.

"Yes, it was. Worst of all, Moses did not get in either."

"Why not?" the group chorused.

"Because even he disobeyed God," Marcus answered. "Once again when the people and animals were thirsty, God told him to speak to a rock and water would come out of it. But Moses was angry with our people. And instead of merely speaking to the rock, he struck it twice. They got water all right. But God never allowed Moses, as great as he was, to enter the wonderful land. (That rock spoke of Christ. See 1 Corinthians 10:4.) The sin of Moses (disobeying God) and the sin of the people (not believing God) were equally serious."

Show Illustration #12

The group was silent before Marcus concluded. "God did allow Moses to stand on a high hill and look at the land. Then God put him to sleep and buried him. (Do you see his grave in the foreground of the illustration?) No one knows to this day where he is buried. What a difference between Moses and the Lord Jesus! The Lord Jesus always obeyed His Father perfectly. And because God the Father was well pleased with His Son, He brought Christ back from the tomb. And today He is living with God in Heaven. The Lord Jesus proved by His resurrection that He is far greater than Moses."

It was sin that caused Moses and the people of God to miss out on the good things God had for them. And sin will keep you from having all that God wants you to have. If you refuse to believe that Jesus is the Son of God and refuse to receive Him as your Saviour, that is sin. Without the Saviour you can't have eternal life. If you are a disobedient Christian, you can't have the joy God wants you to have. Will you tell God right now how you have disobeyed Him and ask His forgiveness? Will you promise to do what He wants you to do?

Lesson 4
JESUS CHRIST, FOREVER THE SAME

Scripture to be studied: Luke 24:13-53; John 20:19-31

The *aim* of the lesson: To show the superiority of Christ.

What your students should *know*: That the Old Testament Scriptures (as well as the New) speak of Christ.

What your students should *feel*: A desire to study God's Word and learn what it teaches about Christ.

What your students should *do*:

Saved: Worship the Lord Jesus with the words of Thomas, "My Lord and my God."

Unsaved: Place all their trust in the risen Son of God.

Lesson outline (for the teacher's and students' notebooks):

1. The risen Lord reveals the meaning of Old Testament Scriptures (Luke 24:13-29).
2. The risen Lord reveals Himself to His own (Luke 24:30-45).
3. The entire Word of God speaks of Christ the Lord (Exodus 12:3-11; Leviticus 23:5; 1 Corinthians 5:7; 1 Peter 1:19; Genesis 6:1–8:22).
4. Jesus Christ, forever the same (John 20:19-31; Hebrews 13:8).

The verse to be memorized:

Jesus Christ the same yesterday, and to day, and forever.
(Hebrews 13:8)

NOTE TO THE TEACHER

This particular lesson is not from the book of Hebrews. However, the truths of Hebrews are taught in this account of our Lord's appearances after His resurrection. In our first three lessons we have seen the importance of prophets, angels and Moses. They were messengers of God the Father. In this lesson we see them as messengers of God the Son.

THE LESSON

Suppose we were going to act out some of the Bible happenings. Which would you rather be: a prophet, an angel, or Moses? Why? (*Teacher:* Encourage class discussion.)

Prophets and angels and Moses are of interest to all of us. They were particularly important to the Jewish Christians who received a letter from God the Holy Spirit. Today we'll turn to the closing chapter of the Book of Luke. These messengers of God mentioned in the opening of the book of Hebrews, are messengers also of Someone else. Listen closely!

Have you ever walked seven miles? (*Teacher:* Give example of this distance in your local area.) How long did it take you? Did it seem like a long walk? If you were happy, you enjoyed the walk. If you were unhappy, the walk seemed endless.

1. THE RISEN LORD REVEALS THE MEANING OF OLD TESTAMENT SCRIPTURES
Luke 24:13-29

One day almost 2,000 years ago, two people walked seven miles. They were returning home from the city of Jerusalem. They had enjoyed seeing their friends in the city. They had enjoyed worshiping God in the beautiful temple.

Other years as they returned, they talked over the news from each friend. That made it seem like a short walk. But this year, oh, how different! Each step was an effort. They walked slowly and talked softly. They felt great unhappiness inside.

Suddenly, another joined them. Immediately He asked, "Why are you sad?"

Cleopas, one of the two, answered "Are you a stranger in Jerusalem? Don't you know the things that've happened?"

"What things?" the Stranger asked.

Cleopas answered, "There was a prophet named Jesus of Nazareth. We thought He had come from God. He was mighty in all He did and said. Many were sure He was Christ [the Messiah], the One God had promised to send to deliver us. We thought He was the One who would save our people from the Roman invaders who are occupying our land. Only a week ago He rode a colt into Jerusalem. The people shouted, 'Blessed is the King who comes in the name of the Lord.' (Luke 19:38) He accepted their praise. And we were certain God's promised One had come."

Cleopas added sadly, "The Jewish leaders arrested Jesus and turned Him over to the Romans. They condemned Him to death and crucified Him. Today is the third day since these things were done. Now something strange has happened. Some women went to the tomb where Jesus was buried. But the tomb was empty. An angel said, 'He is not here. He is risen, as He said. Come, see the place where the Lord lay. And go quickly and tell His disciples.'"

Show Illustration #13

Cleopas continued, "Later two of His disciples ran to the tomb. But they didn't see Jesus."

"You foolish men!" the Stranger said. "Why are you so slow to believe what the prophets have said? Christ had to go through these things before coming into His shining greatness. Listen to what Moses said about Christ. Listen to what the prophets said about Him." The Stranger spoke on and on from the Old Testament Scriptures. The travelers were amazed at the number of messages about Christ which Moses and the prophets had given.

What He said made their hearts beat faster. Without realizing it, it was almost evening and they were home. When the Stranger seemed to be going farther, they asked Him, "Will you stay with us?"

2. THE RISEN LORD REVEALS HIMSELF TO HIS OWN
Luke 24:30-45

He accepted their invitation. While they were eating supper together, He took the bread and gave thanks for it, broke it and gave it to them.

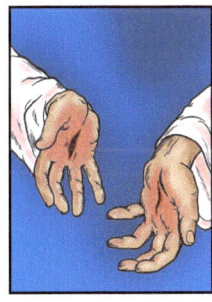

Show Illustration #14

That moment they recognized Him. It was the Lord Jesus Himself! He was alive!

Just as suddenly as He had joined them on the road, He vanished. They were alone. But how different they felt! Their sadness was gone. They were filled with joy.

"We were warm and happy when He talked with us along the road!" Cleopas exclaimed. "It was wonderful how He explained the Scriptures to us!"

Although it was night, they decided to return immediately to Jerusalem. Now their feet seemed to have wings!

By the time they found the disciples, they were breathless. One of the disciples greeted them saying, "The Lord is risen! Peter has seen Him!"

Cleopas responded, "We saw Him, too. He joined us on the way home. He taught us what Moses and the prophets said about Himself in the Scriptures. But we did not recognize Him. Not until He broke bread and gave thanks in our house. Then we saw it was indeed Jesus Christ the Lord. He's alive!"

At that moment, Jesus Himself appeared and said, "Peace to you."

Each held his breath. All were certain it was a spirit. But the Lord said, "Handle Me and see. For a spirit does not have flesh and bones as I have." And He showed them the wound holes in his hands and feet. To help them understand that His body was real, He asked for food and ate it. He was really alive!

Then Jesus said to them, "I told you these things would happen while I was with you. Everything written about Me in the Law of Moses and in the prophets and the Psalms had to happen as they said they would happen." And He made them able to understand the Old Testament Scriptures. (See Luke 24:45; John 2:22.)

3. THE ENTIRE WORD OF GOD SPEAKS OF CHRIST THE LORD
Exodus 12:3-11; Leviticus 23:5; 1 Corinthians 5:7; 1 Peter 1:19; Genesis 6:1-8:22

Show Illustration #15

What did the Lord Jesus teach about Himself? If we look carefully and prayerfully, we can see Christ in many, many pages of the Old Testament. For example, for hundreds of years Jewish people gave lambs as sacrifices for their sins. We have no way of knowing how many millions of lambs died as substitutes for the sinners who offered them. Each sinner brought a perfect lamb to the house of God. He laid his hands on the lamb's head to admit he had sinned. It was his way of transferring his guilt from himself to the lamb. The priest killed the lamb and God forgave the sinner. God had commanded the people to do this. And He gave the command through His servant, Moses. Every lamb that died was a picture of the Lord Jesus Christ, the perfect Lamb of God, who took upon Himself the sins of all the world. (Remember: Moses lived about 1,400 years before Christ.)

There are many other events recorded in the Old Testament which tell something of Christ though they happened long, long before He came. For example, God told Noah (who lived before Moses) that He would destroy the earth with a flood. (The flood was God's punishment for the wickedness of the people.) There was only one way to escape the punishment, God said. "Build a boat, and I will tell you how," God explained. "Only those who are in the boat will be safe."

True to His word, God sent a terrible flood. And everyone on earth was drowned–everyone except Noah and his family. The boat took the punishment and lashing of the storm for those who were safely inside. The people were safe because they were in the boat. Noah's boat is a picture of Christ's taking the punishment for the sins of the world. All who have their trust in Him are safe. (It was Moses who wrote the book of Genesis, in which we have the account of Noah and the flood.)

There are many, many such pictures of Christ in the Old Testament Scriptures. We will see some of them when we study that part of the Bible. We aren't told exactly what Christ taught the two with whom He walked. Nor do we know exactly what He taught the disciples later that night. But we do know He showed them things which Moses and the prophets had written about Him.

4. JESUS CHRIST, FOREVER THE SAME
John 20:19-31; Hebrews 13:8

One of the disciples, Thomas, was absent when the Lord Jesus taught the others on resurrection night. The disciples told him later, "We have seen the Lord."

Thomas replied, "I will not believe that. Not until I see the scars made by the nails. I will not believe until I put my finger into the marks of the nails. I will not believe until I put my hand into His side."

The next Sunday night all the disciples, including Thomas, were together. The doors were locked. Suddenly the Lord Jesus stood among them. "Peace to you," He said. Turning directly to Thomas, He added, "Look at the marks of the nails in My hands. Put your hand into the spear-hole in My side. Do not doubt. Believe!"

Thomas exclaimed, "My Lord and my God!"

At that moment He understood that the Lord Jesus Christ is indeed God the Son. He, the living Lord, was One with the Father from the very beginning. In the words of the verse we have been memorizing, Jesus Christ is "the same yesterday and today and forever."

The Lord Jesus taught the disciples: "It is written [in the Old Testament Scriptures] that Christ should suffer and be raised from the dead after three days. These truths must be preached. People must confess their sins and turn from them. Then they will be forgiven. This must be preached to all nations beginning here in Jerusalem. You are to tell what you have seen."

Show Illustration #16

Not long after this the Lord Jesus ascended and went back to His Father God in Heaven. As He had commanded, the disciples began to tell the Good News. One of the disciples, Peter, preached to a tremendous crowd. He explained that they could be set free from their chains of sin by placing their trust in the crucified, resurrected Son of God. (See Acts 2:23-24, 32-38.) And about 3,000 people turned to the Lord Jesus, the Lamb of God, who had paid the penalty for their sins.

That was a wonderful day. And it was only the beginning. For almost 2,000 years men and women, young and old, have been sharing the same Good News with others. Have you done this? Have you told friends or relatives that Christ died for their sins? Have you explained that He was buried and rose again the third day? If you have not done so, will you promise the Lord Jesus right now that you will give His message to others? He says to you as He said to His early disciples: "All power is given unto Me in Heaven and in earth. You go, therefore, and teach all nations…and, lo, I am with you always." (See Matthew 28:18-20.)

If you are one who has never believed that the Lord Jesus Christ is the Son of God and have never placed your trust in Him, will you do it right now? Remember, He loves you. He died for you. He, the risen, living Lord, wants you for Himself.

www.ingramcontent.com/pod-product-compliance
Lightning Source LLC
Chambersburg PA
CBHW060803090426
42736CB00002B/134